Explaining Cryptocurrency

A Complete Guide To Understanding Blockchain And Cryptos And How to Make Money With Bitcoin Trading

Joshua Kratter

Disclaimer Notice:

Please note the information contained within this document is for educational and entertainment purposes only. All effort has been executed to present accurate, up-to-date, and reliable, complete information. No warranties of any kind are declared or implied. Readers acknowledge that the author is not engaging in the rendering of legal, financial, medical, or professional advice. The content within this book has been derived from various sources. Please consult a licensed professional before attempting any techniques outlined in this book. By reading this document, the reader agrees that under no circumstances is the author responsible for any losses, direct or indirect, which are incurred as a result of the use of the information contained within this document, including, but not limited to, — errors, omissions, or inaccuracies.

Table of Contents

Introduction

Cryptocurrencies are a new concept in the global economy. They exist only for approximately five years, and they have already attracted a lot of attention. Especially since the year 2013, they experience turbulent changes in their exchange rates. The cryptocurrencies belong to the group of virtual currencies. We can consider cryptocurrency as a digital medium of Exchange based on cryptography principles, allowing the performance of secure, decentralized, and distributed economic transactions.

Theoretical foundations of cryptocurrencies were outlined by Chaum for the first time in 1983 already. The cryptocurrencies integrate electronic virtual money with principles of cryptography. The basic principle of cryptocurrency is that no individual (or organization) may accelerate or significantly abuse a given currency production. Typically only a certain predefined amount of cryptocurrency is collectively produced by the entire cryptocurrency system. The rate of production is set by a value defined in prior and is publicly known. The cryptocurrencies allow virtually costless transfers of cryptocurrency units (referred to as coins) between client applications via a peer-to-peer computer network.

The most famous cryptocurrency and the first to be introduced was Bitcoin in 2009. It was designed by a person or a group of persons hiding under the pseudonym Satoshi Nakamoto. Two types of Bitcoin users exist ordinary users and so-called Bitcoin miners. Ordinary users of Bitcoin use digital Wallets similar to electronic banking applications. The Wallet is software for the management of Bitcoin cash, thus sending and receiving payments in bitcoins. Bitcoins exist only as information in files on a computer or a mobile device. Access to these files is restricted to the private key holder, which is used to secure the money. If the computer's file system is damaged or the wallet file is inadvertently deleted, then the wallet file is lost, and the bitcoins it contained are lost forever (in case the wallet file was not backed up). Although Wallet's public address still exists, it can only be accessed by the private key, deleted. Unless one breaks the very secure encryption built into the system, it would not be possible to recover the lost coins. Breaking encryption used by the Bitcoin network by force is virtually impossible promptly.

The mining is the process of new Bitcoins creation, and miners perform it. Miners are the second group of Bitcoin users, and they are solving the artificial mathematical problem by dedicating their computational power to the Bitcoin network. The mining is used to confirm waiting transactions by including them in the Blockchain. The Blockchain is created every 10 minutes in the case of Bitcoin. So every payment in Bitcoins is confirmed in time of 10 minutes. It enforces a chronological order in the Blockchain, protects the network's neutrality, and allows different computers to agree on the system's state. For the transactions to be confirmed, they must be packed in a block that fits very strict cryptographic rules verified by the network. These rules prevent previous blocks from being modified because doing so would invalidate all following blocks. Mining also represents a competitive lottery that prevents any individual from easily adding new blocks consecutively in the Blockchain. So no individuals can control what is included in the Blockchain or replace parts of the Blockchain to roll back their payments. The creation of blocks is proof of mining's work system, so the data are costly and time-consuming to create according to requirements. Bitcoin uses the SHA2-256 cryptographic algorithm as a proof of work mechanism during transaction confirmation. Some cryptocurrencies (e.g., Peercoin) also employ a proof of stake mechanism. The proof of stake mechanism means that fractions of cryptocurrency units are assigned to their holders as a reward for holding the cryptocurrency, which can be considered an analogy of interest.

Since the introduction of Bitcoin, tens of other cryptocurrencies have emerged, the most are based on similar specifications as Bitcoin, which represents the first fully implemented cryptocurrency protocol. The second most popular cryptocurrency Litecoin uses the scrypt algorithm as a proofof-work and has faster transaction confirmations (2.5 minutes). Most cryptocurrencies gradually introduce new currency units until reaching a maximum preset cap of the total amount of currency that will ever be created. The maximum cap of cryptocurrency aims to assure scarcity, similar to the case of precious metals. It also should prevent hyperinflation [6]. On the contrary, some cryptocurrencies might experience hyper deflation as the amount of the currency in circulation will approach its preset finite cap.

All currently existing cryptocurrencies are pseudonymous, so they provide a very high degree of anonymity. Therefore cryptocurrencies are less prone to be confiscated by law enforcement institutions. These facts make cryptocurrencies very attractive to the black market. The case of the Silk Road is infamous. It was an e-marketplace used for drug dealing (and another black-market trading), and it was accepting payments in cryptocurrencies.

However, since the introduction of cryptocurrencies, they continually gain attention (positive or negative) from the media and public, especially during the fast price rise of Bitcoin and Litecoin during the year of 2013

Chapter 1: The Basics of Cryptocurrencies

Our research aimed at investigating basic aspects of cryptocurrencies that might influence their prices. The price of cryptocurrency reflects the trust of users in a given currency and its future development.

Cryptocurrencies bring to their user's freedom of payments. They provide the possibility to send and receive any amount of money quickly anywhere in the world at any time. Users of cryptocurrencies are not limited spatially or in time when realizing their payments, so their users are in full control of their money.

Cryptocurrency payments are processed with no fees or extremely small fees. In Bitcoin, users may include fees with transactions to receive priority processing, which results in faster confirmation of transactions by the network. Additionally, merchant processors exist to assist merchants in processing transactions, converting bitcoins to fiat currency, and depositing funds directly into merchants' bank accounts daily. These services are based on Bitcoin, so that they can be offered much lower fees than with PayPal or credit card networks.

All information concerning the cryptocurrency money supply is readable and available in the Blockchain for anybody to verify and use in real-time, so cryptocurrencies are transparent. Furthermore, no individual or organization can control or manipulate the cryptocurrency protocol because they are cryptographically secured.

Cryptocurrency payments can be made without personal information linked to the transaction. This offers strong protection against identity theft and almost full anonymity. Cryptocurrency users can also protect their money by encryption and backing up their wallets. Also, merchants can't hide any charges, as can happen with other payment methods. The cryptocurrency transactions are secure, irreversible. This protects merchants from losses caused by fraud or fraudulent chargebacks. This allows merchants to have lower fees, enlarge markets, and decrease administrative costs.

On the other hand, the total value of cryptocurrencies in circulation and the number of businesses accepting them are very small compared to classic fiat currencies. Therefore, a relatively small number of trades or events can significantly affect the price of cryptocurrencies. This volatility might decrease as cryptocurrency markets and technologies will mature.

Most of the cryptocurrencies and their software are still in development with many incomplete features. New tools, features, and services might still be developed. Also, many people are still unaware of cryptocurrencies. Both users and businesses accept cryptocurrencies because they want to utilize their advantages, but their numbers remain small and still need to grow to benefit from network effects.

While the total supply of cryptocurrency is predetermined and gradually increases over time with mining, total demand after it may vary dramatically. However, the supply of cryptocurrency on an e-market is not equal to its total supply. It only reflects the amounts of cryptocurrency that market subjects are willing to sell at given prices at a given moment via e-markets.

Prices in official currencies are directly set by demand and supply on e-markets only for two of the most popular cryptocurrencies: Bitcoin and Litecoin. Other cryptocurrencies are directly interchangeable on e-markets only for Bitcoin or Litecoin, respectively. Therefore their exchange rate is strongly influenced also by changes in Bitcoin or Litecoin exchange rates.

Other major aspects that influence the exchange rate of cryptocurrency are its acceptance and usability in various applications. Bitcoin is the most widely accepted cryptocurrency in many cases on the web and brick-and-mortar businesses and merchants.

Many legal official sites accept payments or donations in Bitcoins (or Litecoins). However, in addition to that, many sites merchandising unofficial or even illegal goods (drugs, firearms, etc.) accept it. The main reasons are easy transfers and their almost complete anonymity of cryptocurrency transactions. Logically subjects acting on the black market want to remain anonymous.

Also, the availability of cryptocurrency is an important issue. The easiness of purchasing or exchanging for classical currency into cryptocurrency and vice versa allows better possibilities to use cryptocurrencies. Consequently, it influences their exchange rates. In the case of Bitcoin, there are already ATMs for Bitcoin purchases available in some countries, which use exchange rate from one of the major e-markets allowing cryptocurrency exchange with a small fee covering the

ATMs costs of maintenance and operation. This increases the availability of Bitcoin between wide populations. However, the main source of cryptocurrency remains mining and direct trading on electronic markets.

Furthermore, legislation changes in many countries positively or negatively influence the possibility of using cryptocurrency in legal money transactions. In some countries, legislative arrangements induced by possible illegal cryptocurrency transactions brought restrictions to cryptocurrencies in a particular country. However, this legislation's influence on illegal transactions would be lower because they already are out of a given country's law system for another reason than new legislation restricting cryptocurrency usage.

Awareness about cryptocurrency affects both positively or negatively its exchange rate. Higher awareness of Bitcoin made it very popular last year, partially contributing to its enormous price in 2013. This also affected many other cryptocurrencies, mainly because they are interchangeable with Bitcoin.

All these aspects influence the use of cryptocurrency and its final exchange rate to normal currencies. Together they generate trust in a given cryptocurrency. The higher trust brings the more stable and higher price of the cryptocurrency to the market. We can summarize these aspects of cryptocurrencies into the following basic aspects:

A. Volatility

Volatility represents a measure of the intensity of price changes of a given investment. High volatility might cause serious problems with a given investment.

While considering the cryptocurrency, the main problem caused by the volatility is that of a deflationary bias. With more and more people wanting access to a limited number of cryptocurrencies, its value will be pushed upwards. Therefore, things become cheaper for those that have cryptocurrency in possession. Deflation encourages cash hoarding rather than spending, and it is incorporated directly into the basic principles of current cryptocurrencies. High increases in cryptocurrency values encourage its users to hold cryptocurrency further and avoid its use. For example, O'Brien, at this point, suggests that cryptocurrency ceases to be a currency and becomes a virtual commodity.

On the other hand, big decreases in cryptocurrency's value encourage its holders to sell out their cryptocurrency and buy more stable traditional currencies or commodities. This leads to even greater decreases of cryptocurrency rates as long as their sell-out increases cryptocurrency supply on the market, and sellers tend to sell cryptocurrency at a still lower and lower price. In traditional currencies, central banks avoid these effects and assure currency stability, while cryptocurrencies lack any form of central banking.

However, the high volatility is not for cryptocurrency users, only the bad news. Even short-term speculations might bring high earnings to cryptocurrency speculators. This fact, along with thehigh growth of cryptocurrency exchange rates, attracted even more speculators. It led to even bigger price growth and the creation of price bubbles. Although users holding cryptocurrencies, who purchased (or mined) it sooner in the past before the volatile year of 2013 might have recorded above 1000 percent earnings.

Having a volatile currency means that businesses can't plan or budget effectively, and the chaos that this could cause would be too much of a risk for most, even if sometimes they came out ahead. Nobody knows how much stuff a bitcoin will be able to buy in a day, a week, or a month – there are no fundamentals to speak of.

High demand after cryptocurrencies made them very volatile with predominant growth of exchange rate. These effects are transferred from Bitcoin and Litecoin into other cryptocurrencies thanks to their interchangeability only via the medium of Bitcoin or Litecoin. The recorded extreme volatility of cryptocurrencies suggests them only for risk-takers, considering them as an investment possibility.

B. Awareness

The awareness of cryptocurrency affects its users' count and, therefore, the stability of its exchange rate. The higher awareness of a given cryptocurrency means its more potential users. A very big role in the field of awareness plays the media. High media coverage of Bitcoin's price rally drew the attention of numerous additional speculators, who then invested in Bitcoin and participated in its enormous growth of the price. Besides all forms of media, word of mouth also increases the awareness of cryptocurrencies and contributes to increased cryptocurrency users numbers.

C. Availability

Another important aspect of cryptocurrencies is their availability for use. Availability is influenced by the easiness of purchasing and their interchangeability for official standard currencies. This is enabled by private electronic markets available to the general public.

Several subjects accepting payments in a given cryptocurrency also reflects its availability and usability. The number of merchants accepting some cryptocurrency (Bitcoin mainly) is increasing, but they face the problem of the high volatility of cryptocurrencies, so in most cases, they do not keep cryptocurrency for a longer period and change for standard currency. On the other hand, higher availability brings a higher and more stable exchange rate of cryptocurrency thanks to an increased number of users of a given cryptocurrency, slowing rate changes, and decreasing its volatility in time.

Further, the speed of transactions and their confirmations processes makes cryptocurrency more available and practical for payments in an electronic environment.

C. Anonymity

All cryptocurrency payments between anonymous sides are hardly traceable. This fact is the main reason for their usage in criminal operations. Very hard transaction traceability and no central guaranty of currency are the main reasons for criticism and legislation restrictions of cryptocurrencies.

Governments and security authorities are also afraid of virtually untraceable transactions connected with criminal financing activities or terrorist organizations. Cryptocurrencies with virtually anonymous transactions are potentially very useful for such financial transfers to terrorists from their sponsors. This lack of transfers' identification led to multiple legislation adjustments and arrangements for cryptocurrency usage restrictions in recent years.

On the other hand, legal users might also prefer anonymous transactions due to privacy intrusions by any third party not involved in the transaction. After recent cases of disclosure of governmental tracking of private communications, are privacy concerns even more understandable?

So anonymity of cryptocurrency affects the usage of cryptocurrencies both positively and negatively.

D. Legislation influence

Before the year 2009, not a single national legislation contained the term of cryptocurrency. Since then, an increasing amount of money transferred in cryptocurrency has forced policymakers in many countries to issue a recommendation or create laws regarding cryptocurrency in the national economy. Broader allowance of cryptocurrency usage supports its usage and generates bigger trust in it. However, most countries did not allow the use of cryptocurrency or concede to them the currency status. This action restrained the possibility of its usage in the legal economy. However, it keeps its status of the safe and anonymous medium of Exchange in the illegal economy.

Any illegal transactions by cryptocurrencies as payments for illegal commodities and services are affected by valid cryptocurrency legislation only to a minor extent as long as these transactions are already part of activity violating some other laws with greater criminal consequences.

19

The area of cryptocurrency introduction process rules lacks the legislation treatment. Although cryptocurrencies are independent, multiple pre-mining or pump-and-dump schemes during the introduction of some cryptocurrencies negatively affected the trust in all cryptocurrencies

Chapter 2: How Crypto-Currencies Work

The source codes and technical controls that support and secure cryptocurrencies are highly complex. However, laypeople are more than capable of understanding the basic concepts and becoming informed cryptocurrency users.

Functionally, most cryptocurrencies are variations on Bitcoin, the first widely used cryptocurrency. Like traditional currencies, cryptocurrencies' express value in units – for instance, you can say, "I have 2.5 Bitcoin," just as you'd say, "I have $2.50."

Several concepts govern cryptocurrencies' values, security, and integrity.

What Problems Could Cryptocurrency Solve?

Cryptocurrencies are often looked at as two things: an investment tool and a way to ensure transactions remain discreet.

Nevertheless, what if we told you it has the potential to be more? That its design properties mean it could be used as a tool to solve some of the world's biggest issues?

Take, for example, its blockchain technology, which can record transactions without a middle person (like a bank) and a virtually un-hackable process. Something like this could be used to stamp out a human error or even corruption when making monetary transactions.

So, let's look at some other things that could be fixed up with some of these technological designs:

Inflation.

Simply put, inflation is when your cash is worth less than it used to be over time. It can happen when your government prints more money; the worth of your $20 note loses a bit of value because another five (or five million) have just been circulated. What happens like to your rare collectibles (think shiny Pokémon cards). If they become common, they're not worth much, but everyone is willing to pay a bit more to get them when they're extremely hard to come by.

However, with cryptocurrencies, the supply is finite, unlike fiat currencies (traditional money backed by a government like the Australian dollar). As of July 2019, only 80 percent of the world's Bitcoin has been made available. According to expert Daniel Garnsey from crypto-trading platform NCX, this means "Bitcoin is protected from inflation caused in fiat currency markets [where] governments simply [print] more money." Seeing how inflation can adversely affect economies by increasing the cost of goods and lowering the purchasing power of people's wages, limiting inflation is a step in the right direction.

Digital voting.

Blockchain, a technology introduced when the first crypto (Bitcoin) was created, can be utilized in many applications. One proposed suggestion is that blockchain technology could allow for a robust digital voting system in many democracies worldwide.

As Garnsey says, "Blockchain technology could change the way countries elect leaders in the future as it can reduce the time and cost involved in the election process."

It could work by recording votes made by an eligible citizen after verification. Votes would then be hosted on the private Blockchain after their identity has been verified.

However, some experts warn that the technology is not ready just yet to take on the monumental responsibility of managing the votes and determining a country's government. Until then, it's paper and pencil for you!

Equality In Money Management.

An obvious advantage of cryptocurrency is its feature to cut out the middle person, a role that would typically belong to a traditional bank. There are a few reasons you might want to favor cryptos over banks. For starters, banks close down during holidays and offer limited services. Also, transferred money can sometimes take days to show up in your account. They're also not tied to a single location.

"Cryptocurrency wallets are simple and fast to establish and operate on a global scale," Garnsey offers instead.

There's also a major added benefit for women in Saudi Arabia, where they cannot hold their bank accounts without a male guardian's input.

With the use of cryptocurrencies, these women could bypass using a traditional bank to hold their money, meaning they have the freedom to manage their funds. Some reports have suggested women in Afghanistan have already been getting paid for their work in cryptocurrency.

Stop Future Global Financial Crises.

If you were alive back in 2008, you might've heard a thing or two about the Global Financial Crisis (GFC). If you haven't, watch Hollywood's take on it, The Big Short, and seethe with anger.

The TL;DR of it all was that some big boys in the finance world realized banks were playing pretty loose with the rules and giving out loans to people who could not afford them. This (among many other dodgy things) undermined the entire global economy, forcing millions out of work and, in some cases, out of their homes.

This would've likely been avoided with cryptocurrency, as blockchains tend to be a far more transparent system than the private investment firms offered. It could've offered real-time insights into the house of cards that was about to tumble down and given politicians and lawmakers a chance at avoiding the eventual catastrophe that would eventuate.

"Transparency is a major benefit of a cryptocurrency transaction," says Garnsey.

"Once written to the blockchain, it can't be changed, which provides a trustless environment of publicly available information."

Stamp out embezzling and improve trust in charitable donations.

As mentioned, with blockchain technology, financial transparency within private companies is much easier to achieve.

However, arguably, it's most important for charities that face a lack of public trust.

Coins like AidCoin are designed to stamp out illegitimate charities and demonstrate how cryptos can be used for the common good. They aim to help donators keep track of where their money is going and force charities to be more transparent.

"Charities can take advantage of the transparency benefits of the blockchain," says Garnsey.

"This has the potential to change the way not-for-profit organizations operate in the future."

Chapter 3: The "king" of Crypto: The Bitcoin

From the definition given directly by the creator Satoshi Nakatomo, that is the most important forum for the Bitcoin community "There'snothing to relate it (bitcoin) to."

What Is A Bitcoin (BTC)

Bitcoin is "is the first digital decentralized currency" as it can be read in the bitcoin.org website and is defined as a "purely peer-to-peer version of electronic cash that would allow online payments to be sent directly from one party to another without going through a financial institution." by Satoshi Nakatomo in a paper talking about it.

In these multiples, basic definitions are clear that the single word "Bitcoin" has a lot to tell. First of all, the word Bitcoin with "B" capital letter is the whole network of payments, where there is traded a new kind of decentralized value, that means that there is not an entity that controls the emission and regulates it: the bitcoin with lowercase "b."

The creation of this new type of currency arises from the need to disengage from the traditional online payments method, which in addition to the two parties that have to make an exchange includes a trusted third party: financial institutions. These act as guarantors to avoid the problem of double-spending that consists of spending the same currency twice as being digital. In this regard, the bitcoin network offers a solution to this double-spending problem by providing an electronic payment system no longer based on trust (and therefore on financial institutions) but on cryptography, "implementing a mechanism of confirmation and maintaining a universal ledger (called "blockchain") cash monetary system."

Therefore, the problem of the necessary control for the normal exchanges in legal value is also solved in this case: in fact, the data are diffused and distributed in the network and guaranteed through the adhesion of every single user to a unique protocol, compliant and difficult to force despite the open-source nature of the Bitcoin network.

At this point, it becomes important to clarify some points related to the key concept of decentralization, as both the software and the protocol of adhesion of individual users have been created by the creator Satoshi Nakamoto and this could generate doubts and perplexities as one might think that he could act as a central authority. The problem is dispelled considering that, as mentioned previously, the nature of the software is open-source and free: in fact, every single user can bring improvements to the protocol although the latter is difficult to force deep because each node is then free to choose which a version of the software to use as long as it complies with the rules and the protocol used by the other nodes. This last point is of fundamental importance because it highlights the aspect of consensus between users and developers for the network to work, and this also makes it difficult to centralize this system and to regulate it.

To conclude then it can be said how Bitcoin can be defined as a new innovative payment a system whose control is no longer in the hands of a central authority that regulates everything but in which thanks to the diffusion of specific software and protocol are possible transactions of virtual currency not regulated by a third party that acts as guarantor.

Bitcoin Advantages:

Freedom in Payment

With Bitcoin, it is possible to be able to send and get money anywhere in the world at any given time. You do not have to worry about crossing borders, rescheduling for bank holidays or any other limitations one might think will occur when transferring money. You are in control of your money with Bitcoin. There is no central the authority figure in the Bitcoin network.

Control and Security

Allowing users to be in control of their transactions help keep Bitcoin safe for the network. • Merchants cannot charge extra fees on anything without being noticed. They must talk with the consumer before adding any charges. Payments in Bitcoin can be made and finalized without personal information being tied to the transactions.

Because personal information is kept hidden from prying eyes, Bitcoin protects against identity theft. Bitcoin can be backed up and encrypted to ensure the safety of your money.

Information is Transparent

With the Blockchain, all finalized transactions are available for everyone to see; however, personal information is hidden. Your public address is what is visible; however, your personal information is not tied to this.

Anyone at any time can verify transactions in the Bitcoin blockchain. Bitcoin protocol cannot be manipulated by any person, organization, or government. This is due to Bitcoin being cryptographically secure.

Very Low Fees

Currently, there are either no fees or very low fees within Bitcoin payments.

With transactions, users might include fees to process the transactions faster. The higher the fee, the more priority it gets within the network, and the quicker it gets processed.

Digital Currency exchanges help merchants process transactions by converting bitcoins into fiat currency. These services generally have lower fees than credit cards and PayPal.

Fewer Risks for Merchants

Because Bitcoin transactions cannot be reversed, do not carry with them personal information, and are secure, merchants are protected from potential losses that might occur from fraud.

With Bitcoin, merchants can do business where crime rates and fraud rates may be high. This is because it is very hard to cheat or con anyone in Bitcoin due to the public ledger, otherwise known as the Blockchain.

Now that we've covered the basic advantages, we can move on to the disadvantages. Three main ones need to be pointed out. This is so you can get an overall idea of what to expect with Bitcoin.

Bitcoin Disadvantages:

Lack of Awareness & Understanding

Fact is, many people are still unaware of digital currencies and Bitcoin. People need to be educated about Bitcoin to be able to apply it to their lives.

Networking is a must to spread the word on Bitcoin. Businesses are accepting bitcoins because of the advantages, but the the list is relatively small compared to physical currencies.

Companies like Tiger direct and Overstock accepting Bitcoin as payment is great. However, if they do not have a knowledgeable staff that understands digital currencies, how will they help customers understand and use Bitcoin for transactions?

The workers need to be educated on Bitcoin so that they can help the customers. This will take some time and effort. Otherwise, what is the benefit of such large companies accepting Bitcoin if its staff doesn't even know what digital currencies are?

Risk and Volatility

Bitcoin has volatility mainly because there is a limited amount of coins and the demand for them increases by each passing day.

However, it is expected that the volatility will decrease as more time goes on. As more businesses, media, and trading centers begin to accept Bitcoin, its' price will eventually settle down. Currently,

Bitcoin's price bounces every day mainly due to current events that are related to digital currencies.

Still Developing

Bitcoin is still at its infancy stage with incomplete features that are in development. To make the digital currency more secure and accessible, new features, tools and services are currently being developed. Bitcoin has some growth to do before it comes to its full and final potential.

This is because Bitcoin is just starting, and it needs to work out its problems just like how any currency in its beginning stage would need to.

Chapter 4:
Characteristics of
Cryptocurrencies

Cryptocurrencies are digital currencies independent of any central unit, which use cryptography to verify transactions and adjust the issuance of new currency units.

The main characteristics of bitcoins (also common with those of other major cryptocurrencies) are:

Decentralization:

It has not been established; any central authority controls it. Many independent entities in decentralized and perform transaction checking distributed manner, so the presence of banks and other subjects regulated is no longer necessary.

It Is Not Subject To Monetary Policies:

The absence of a central authority involves also the impossibility that any subject exercises coercive actions on the currency, such as the increase or decrease of currency units in circulation. The money supply is established a priori by the protocol so that it increases Over time up to the maximum set limit of 21 million units.

It Has No Legal Tender:

It is accepted as a means of payment only on a basis voluntary, and therefore cannot be used to pay off obligations pecuniary if the creditor refuses to accept them.

Pseudonym:

Transactions take place between public addresses from which it is practically impossible to trace the real identity of the natural or legal person that processes the virtual currency exchange. But user identity remains unknown until it is revealed during a transaction or in other cases, so these addresses should be used only once for each transaction.

Transparent:

All transactions are recorded in a register open to the public, the Blockchain, which anyone can view. Exploring the Blockchain is possible to know how many bitcoins every single address at any given time, going back to the addresses given to them.

Low Transaction Costs:

The absence of subjects that interfere in transactions reduces the costs. On average, the transactions include a debit to the the sender of 0.0001 BTC (about 0.02 €) as a commission, but the amount may be greater or void depending on certain conditions (it will be discussed later).

Fast And Irreversible Transactions:

Every bitcoin transaction takes on average 10 minutes to be confirmed. These transactions are irreversible that it is impossible to cancel

Chapter 5: How To Store and Use Crypto

There are several ways to get bitcoins, some simple and some more complex. On the other hand, there are always growing businesses, both physical and online, where they can be spent.

However, before thinking of how to get and spend bitcoins, and need to be able to do it to receive, and once received, to be able to keep them safe, without risking losing them or to have them "steal." For this purpose, it is necessary to have a Bitcoin wallet, a wallet electronic which performs the same functions as a portfolio material, that is, the custody of our money, which in this case is digital.

Bitcoin Wallet

Bitcoin wallets are not exactly the equivalent of a current account, though the graphical the interface offered by the various wallet services allows you to know at any time the total of the bitcoin possessed and the movements in and out, as a kind of account statement in real-time.

These are not contained within a portfolio but are stored in a register open to the public, the Blockchain, below specific addresses belonging to different users.

Addresses are reception points and sending and are presented in the form of alphanumeric codes of 33 or 34 characters, generally starting for 1, so as not to contain any user reference, making Bitcoin a pseudonym payment system. The addresses derive using algorithms from other codes, the so-called public keys, and these once again derive through other algorithms from the so-called private keys, so that starting from the address, it is impossible to trace the original public key and from this to the private key.

Through the encryption of digital signatures, only the private key's possession authorizes the user to spend the associated bitcoins at the address derived from it. For this reason, the private key does not have to be rendered public but must be kept in order not to run the risk of someone else taking possession of it.

These wallets store the user's private keys, which allow him to spend the bitcoins associated with the precise address that derives from the public key that its turn derives from the private key in question; this is what happens behind the scenes. The Wallet offers the user an intuitive interface, similar to that of the online banking app that allows him to view the bitcoin balance at his disposal of all the different addresses he has, giving him the possibility to make outgoing transactions towards certain beneficiaries, or to receive payments at a specific address.

When you create a new wallet, one hundred pairs of them are automatically generated private and public keys (a key-pool mechanism), for which the user can use multiple addresses different, to enjoy greater levels of privacy. So, every transaction is registered in the Blockchain, and anyone can see all the movements of an address; if an individual and able to associate an address with physical identity, then for example to bargaining where payment details were exchanged, these can control all the movements, for this reason, change often address is guarantee of greater privacy.

There are different types of portfolios (only a few are mentioned) to choose from, depending on the levels of user convenience, security and complexity desired, type of device used, if smartphones, desktops, and even there is the ability to choose between operating systems:

Desktop Wallet:

it is a software to install on your computer that allows you to store and store private keys on the hard disk. The installation of this software generally requires the download of the entire Blockchain. They are available for different operating systems (Windows, Mac, Linux). The security that guarantees this type of the Wallet can be high, but only if you take the necessary precautions: in fact, if the device is not protected by antivirus or does not provide to protect it or the Wallet has not been encrypted with an appropriate password, the user runs the risk that some hackers steal the private keys from their PC, or anyway if the same was lost or left unattended, anyone would have access to the Wallet and could spend the bitcoins. Finally, it is highly recommended to make periodic backups of the Wallet to recover the private keys if the PC is damaged or lost.

Mobile Wallet:

Wallet applications for smartphones that make it possible to keep, send, or receive bitcoins from your mobile phone quickly and easily. This type of application does not require the download of the entire Blockchain, but only of a part of it, relying on information from other network nodes.

As for desktop wallets, it is recommended to make periodic backups.

Online Wallet:

Service offered by different websites stores private keys, storing them in online servers placed under their protection. In other words, the user entrusts their bitcoins' custody to third parties, in this case, a website. Typically, online wallets are offered on an ancillary basis by exchanges, platforms buying, and selling bitcoins in exchange for traditional currencies.

Considering the unpleasant inconveniences that happened to some of these exchanges in the past, probably this type of Wallet is not the safest, but it is easier and faster to use, as it can be accessed from anywhere device connected to the internet. So, keep a lot of bitcoins in these types of wallets is not particularly suitable, while for small but frequent transactions are undoubtedly the most practical to use.

Paper Wallet:

Private and public keys can be stored directly from the same user in paper support and kept so protected from hackers and possible failures of their electronic devices. . Once you've exported your paper wallet, the public key is not more memorized digitally anywhere, so it is recommended to keep it appropriately and maybe create some copies for security. The address can normally receive payments, but to spend such bitcoins, the user must re-import your private key online or on a software wallet to sign the outgoing transactions. From this point of view, the security offered by a paper wallet. It is very high and works great as a long-term bitcoin deposit but is more complicated to use.

Hardware Wallet:

These are devices created specifically for storing private keys, bitcoin addresses, and other cryptocurrencies. It is not done concerning the other types of wallets entrusting to third parties to conserve the codes; there is no risk that a hacker steals them, and they do not have to be re-imported online or in one software to make outgoing transactions. The hardware wallets are goods minicomputers with a single function, digitally signing transactions with the user's private keys. These usually connect to the computer via USB and safely interact with the software wallet even if the computer is compromised. The user checks the correctness of the address from the computer to send bitcoins and and authorize the transaction by entering a PIN on your hardware wallet, which hackers cannot intercept

Chapter 6: Buying Cryptocurrencies

Once illustrated how to store BTC, it is good to show how they can be obtained. Obviously, the ways to buy them are many, shown below:

Buy Them From People Willing To Sell Them:

Localbitcoins.com is the leading face-to-face exchange website platform and is present in 16263 cities and 248 countries, including Italy.

Who wants to buy bitcoins can decide whether to exchange online, choosing one of the various payment methods (bank transfer, PayPal, Postepay, Skrill, Moneybooker) or arrange a physical meeting with the seller and exchange bitcoins in exchange for cash, in how much you can find offers also relatively close in geographical terms. Face-to-face meetings must take place in places where internet access is available, necessary for processing transactions, while for online exchanges, it is always recommended to check seller feedback.

Another similar platform is a social network that brings together groups of people by areas of interest, including bitcoins. Some of these groups organize periodically meetings, to which it is possible to participate and have direct contact with the topic and with the people of the "community."

Another interesting opportunity is represented by the so-called "Satoshi S quare," which are public events, mainly in large cities where a public square or park is transformed into an open-air bitcoin market. The first was organized by Josh Rossi, as a tribute to "Wall Street," held in New York in May 2013. In addition to facilitating the exchange, these events have contributed to giving public evidence, thus allowing better communication and information.

Buying At Online Exchanges:

Many sites on the web allow bitcoins to purchase for legal tender or other cryptocurrencies. These platforms play the role of market makers by fixing exchange rates to which the exchange buys or sells bitcoins in Exchange for the main traditional currencies or currencies other virtual currencies.

Buying At Bitcoin Atms Is A Much quicker Purchase Or Sale Service Than Exchange Online And Offered By Bitcoin Atms.

The first ATM bitcoin, produced by an American company Robocoin was installed in 2013 at the Waves Coffee House in Vancouver (Canada) and, already in its first day of operation, recorded as many as 81 transactions totaling over $ 10,000. There are currently 3480 bitcoin ATMs in 72 countries, of which 17 in Italy and the number is constantly increasing. In circulation, there are different models, among which the most widespread ones.

These devices are almost always of two types:

1. Unidirectional, that is, they allow to convert only legal currency into bitcoins,

46

2. Bidirectional, the ones that instead allow both to buy and to sell bitcoins in exchange for legal tender.

Compared to the options listed above, that represented by ATMs, bitcoin is more easily and immediately used. If you already own an electronic wallet buy or sell bitcoins can take anywhere from 15 to 30 seconds, while if you were faced with a Robocoin Kiosk or a BitAccess can create a new wallet and buy some bitcoins all in less than 5 minutes, thus reducing the the time required for authentication normally from an online exchange.

In general, the process of buying (or selling) bitcoins through an ATM takes place in the following phases:

1. Verification phase:

This phase is possible, given that not all ATM models in circulation foresee it. The verification can consist of the simple insertion of a code that the machine sends to the user by text message after inserting the mobile number. In the presence of more sophisticated models, it consists of the user's real personal and physical recognition. This is the case of Robocoin Kiosk, which can only be accessed by creating a personal account. The device at the customer's first access capture scans of the identity document or passport, of the face through the palm, while from the second access in then the verification will come by simply placing the palm on the scanner and entering the numeric PIN chosen;

2. Entering the Bitcoin address:

This step is performed by scanning the QR Code6 associated with the electronic wallet in which you want to receive bitcoins or from which you want to withdraw bitcoins in exchange for money.

Some of these ATMs also allow the generation of new addresses at the time of use;

3. Selection of the cash amount:

That you want to change into bitcoin and its insertion into the slot. In the case of two-way ATM's, it is possible to convert bitcoins into legal currency while always depending on the model of the device, and it is also possible to buy other cryptocurrencies;

4. Confirmation of the operation.

Selling goods and services in exchange for bitcoins: currently, this option is more easily negotiated by those who conduct a business. I'm always more numerous stores, both physical and online, accepting bitcoin in payments exchange of goods and services.

The easiest way for a merchant to accept payments in bitcoins from their customers and communicate the address and wait for these make payment with your smartphone. However, they are constantly growing services aimed at simplifying and speeding up foreign currency payment procedures digital.

5. Mining:

It is the activity of validation and registration of bitcoin transactions that happen continuously in the system. This activity is carried out by the nodes of the network that or this the reason they are called miners, and it consists of doing their computer of complex cryptographic problems in a repetitive way, expensive in terms of electricity consumption and equipment wear.

Mining is incentivized by a precise system of rewards, consisting of bitcoins of a new issue in quantity and with times established by the protocol (will be discussed in the next chapter) and represents the only creation and entering of new currency units. Each node works autonomously, simultaneously and in competition with everyone the other nodes to solve the problem first and win the reward.

Alternatively, the nodes can work together in groups called mining pools, sharing their computational strength to get more chance to get rewards, in competition with other autonomous nodes or other groups.

The total computing power of Bitcoin is given by the sum of the powers of all the devices made available by the nodes, and it is important because from this derives the difficulty in cryptographic problems to be solved by miners. This difficulty yes automatically adjusts so that increasing the total power also increases the difficulty and vice versa, ensuring that transaction is always validated within one a certain amount of time (10 minutes), and the rewards are the same donate constantly.

The Bitcoin system solves this double-spending problem cleverly. The transaction that is first added to a valid block candidate, and therefore added to the Blockchain is considered confirmed. The system ceases to process the other one—that is, miners will stop adding the conflicting transaction to their block candidates. Moreover, a minor can't add conflicting transactions to the same block candidate. Such a block would be illegitimate and thus be rejected by all the other network participants.

Where To Use BTC

Bitcoins in particular but also some similar cryptocurrencies can be used for the purchase of goods and services. To find the shops that accept the payment of goods and services with virtual currency, it is useful to consult the coinmap.org website, which includes a map that provides the nearby stores' exact location.

Moreover, it is possible to consult, especially for the Italian market, the QuiBitcoin application, which indicates these stores' positions that accept this type of payment and traces the Bitcoin ATMs already mentioned above. These figures are still few in Italy because of the still rather long transaction times. Many of those who accept this type of payment use the US Bitpay provider and, recently, the new Conio service, which allows the merchant to accept Bitcoin payments and choose whether to receive Bitcoin or Euro in Exchange.

As far as e-commerce is concerned, cryptocurrencies are easier to use: in fact, they are widely used and appreciated by sellers because, as already mentioned above, it has the undeniable advantage of the payment irreversibility (after about 10 minutes for validation operation).

Chapter 7: The "Altcoins"

The fundamental open source feature of the Nakatomi project allowed the participation of many developers who, since the creation of Bitcoin in 2009, have made an essential contribution to software development and the correction of defects such as the vulnerability of the system and then started the creation of similar projects that allowed the creation of the so-called Altcoins.

To date, according to estimates by coinmarketcap.com, there are 1865 cryptocurrencies for a market capitalization equal to 211,732,582,263 USD10, and the number of cryptocurrencies is constantly growing.

Many of these cryptocurrencies use the same basic mechanisms as Bitcoin, while others propose different solutions, uses, and functionalities compared to Nakatomo's initial project.

Among the most important, we find Ethereum, which has four characteristics in common with Bitcoin or has an underlying cryptocurrency, an intrinsic blockchain, a mechanism of decentralization based on proof-of-work and miners who help the network, but the project Ethereum moves towards a diametrically opposite direction concerning the Bitcoin project.

Also, Ethereum's cryptocurrency, Ether (ETH), deviates from the Bitcoin currency because its main use is not the payment of goods or services, nor the fact of being a "digital version" of gold but rather it is similar to a distribution incentive, a sort of fuel crypto, necessary to pay the transaction costs to run the various smart business logic programs that users send to the Blockchain.

Besides to be a network fuel, Ethereum is also marketable as a cryptocurrency on a variety of open trades, but it is expected that appreciation of its value will be more influenced by the quantity and wealth of transaction demand rather than by the action of speculators, as happened with Bitcoin. Also, the Ethereum blockchain was designed to be fully programmable and is more cost-effective than Bitcoin's, being more scalable, a key requirement for the long-term the convenience of a heavily trafficked blockchain. Since it is not focused on carrying out financial transactions, the purpose of the Ethereum blockchain is different from that of the Bitcoin blockchain.

On Ethereum, there are no limits to the size of a block, and the system adjusts dynamically as a whole, as part of its basic design.

Also, Ethereum continues to work to improve the aspects relevant to scalability, and this will have the direct benefit of lowering overall transaction costs. In general, by considering what the desirable characteristics of a blockchain are, they come to mind the following, which are the same characteristics in which Ethereum excels: Programmability, Scalability, Updatability, Management of transactions, Visibility, Convenience, Security, Speed/Performance, High Availability, Extensibility.

Bitcoin Vs. Other Major Cryptocurrencies

Cryptocurrencies are virtual currencies that operate independently of banks and governments but can still be exchanged – or speculated on – just like any physical currency. Launched in 2009, bitcoin was the first decentralized cryptocurrency. Since then, thousands of more cryptocurrencies, known as altcoins, have launched.

While bitcoin remains the market leader, cryptocurrencies including bitcoin cash, bitcoin gold, Ether, Etheroin, Ripple, EOS, stellar (XLM), and NEO could challenge in the future because of rising demand, expanded applications, and technological advances.

Bitcoin (BTC)

The original, and (for now) the biggest by market capitalization. In 2009, Satoshi Nakamoto launched a pseudonym for the mysterious person or group who created it to secure payments across a peer-to-peer network. It aims to eliminate the need for a trusted third party, democratize money, and ensure that transactions are anonymous.

Biggest pro: best-known cryptocurrency
Biggest con: slow transaction speeds, requires specialist mining equipment

Bitcoin cash (BCH)

Bitcoin cash is a standalone digital currency, created as an offshoot of bitcoin in August 2017 by a 'hard fork.' This was in response to the slowdown in bitcoin transaction speeds and the network's inability to reach consensus on proposed upgrades. Bitcoin cash's maximum block size is 8 M.B., compared to 1 M.B. for bitcoin, enabling it to process more transactions each second.

Biggest pro: faster transaction times than bitcoin
Biggest con: requires specialist mining equipment

Ripple (XRP)

Ripple is a cryptocurrency underpinning a payment network called RippleNet – used by major banks and financial institutions, including Santander and American Express. Ripple operates differently from other digital currencies, which has led some to question its credentials as a truly decentralized cryptocurrency.

Biggest pro: lightning-fast transaction speeds
Biggest con: RippleNet can be used without its underlying cryptocurrency, Ripple Stellar (XLM)

Stellar

Stellar is a payment network that operates similarly to RippleNet and can process transactions in multiple currencies. A cryptocurrency underpins it called lumens (XLM), commonly referred to as 'stellar' (including on the I.G. platform). Lumens can be used for payments on the network and play an anti-spam role, as each transaction requires a small transaction fee, which is paid for in the cryptocurrency.

Biggest pro integrates with banks, used to process transactions in multiple currencies
Biggest con: cryptocurrency not as widely recognized as some other

Ether (ETH)

Ether is the cryptocurrency of the Ethereum network, enabling users to code and release their own 'decentralized applications (apps)' and create 'smart' contracts that automatically enforce their clauses. Small amounts of Ether aEtherstroyed as transactions are processed, preventing hackers from spamming the network.

Biggest pro: use beyond cryptocurrency on the Ethereum network, fast transaction speeds

Biggest con: uncapped supply means that it could be inflationary

Litecoin (LTC)

Litecoin is designed to be 'silver to bitcoin's gold,' according to its founder Charlie Lee. And just as the supply of silver outstrips the supply of gold, Litecoin's maximum supply of 84 million coins is four times greater than bitcoin's. There are also some fundamental technological differences between the two.

Biggest pro: fast transaction speeds

Biggest con: low market capitalization compared to bitcoin

EOS (EOS)

EOS is the cryptocurrency of EOS.IO, a blockchain platform that replicates the key functionality of a computer's hardware and operating system. It provides developers with tools and services to build apps, including user accounts, authentication, and databases. Responsibility for processing and other operations is distributed across the network, which its designers claim will enable it to scale to millions of transactions per second in the future.

Biggest pro: integrated with the EOS.IO network, fast transaction speeds

Biggest con: uncapped supply means that it could be inflationary

NEO (NEO)

NEO is the name of both the cryptocurrency and the network it runs on. This network is like Ethereum in that it enables users to create decentralized apps and smart contracts. However, NEO apart is that its network is currently tightly controlled by 'NEO Team,' which require users to have a verifiable identity on the network.

Biggest pro: integrated with the NEO network, compliant with regulations in many jurisdictions
Biggest con: may not be truly decentralized

Chapter 8: The "Blockchain"

The Blockchain is a set of blocks in which a set of subjects makes available to other computer resources such as memory, CPU, band, to make available to a community of users a mainly public database. It exploits peer-to-peer technology and allows anyone to download, thus becoming a "node" of the network. It is essentially the accounting book in which all transactions made in Bitcoin since 2009 are made, made possible by the approval of 50% + 1 of the nodes. These singleblock transactions occur continuously in the system, and on average, every 10 minutes, a new block is produced and attached to the chain so that the blocks are arranged in chronological order starting from the block of origin, the so-called genesis block.

The same mechanism of the chain is also replicated for the transactions contained in the blocks, even if with some difference: in fact, every transaction is not connected to its previous one in chronological order, but to its transaction-input, or the previous exchange, or to the previous exchanges, which provided bitcoins to the receiver so that they could subsequently become the sender in the transaction in question. The Blockchain can be considered a system whose single transaction and proceeding represent smaller and central particles to the outside. The block, which contains many of these transactions, and finally, the multiple blocks containing the history of Bitcoin from its birth. The structure and functioning of the Blockchain represent the main and fundamental technological innovation in the field of distributed systems. Therefore, it is defined as an open system of verification that does not need the banks' approval to carry out a transaction.

Extrapolated from its original context, the Blockchain has been used in all areas in which a the relationship is needed between several people or groups, with considerable success over the years

Risks

Much like any other key innovation, blockchain technology introduces some risks. The following sections will consider some of these risks. As we mentioned in Section 3, we would like to note that this list is non-exhaustive.

Forks

As discussed in Section 1.8, the Bitcoin protocol can be altered if the network participants, or at least a sufficient number, agree on the suggested modification. It can happen (and has happened) that a blockchain splits because various groups cannot agree about a modification. A split that persists is referred to as a "fork." The two best-known examples of persistent splits are the Bitcoin Cash fork and Ethereum's ideological dissent, which resulted in the split to Ethereum and Ethereum Classic.

Energy Wastage

Proof-of-work Mining is expensive, as it uses a great deal of energy. Some criticize Bitcoin and assert that a centralized accounting system is more efficient because consensus can be attained without the allocation of massive amounts of computational power.

From our perspective, however, the situation is not so clear-cut. Centralized payment systems are also expensive. Besides infrastructure and operating costs, one would have to calculate a central bank's explicit and implicit costs. Salary costs should be counted among the explicit costs and the possibility of fraud in the currency monopoly among the implicit costs.

Moreover, many crypto assets use alternative consensus protocols, which do not (solely) rely on on computational resources.

Bitcoin Price Volatility

The price of Bitcoin is highly volatile. This leads us to whether the rigid predetermined supply of Bitcoin is a desirable monetary policy in the sense that it leads to a stable currency. The answer is no because the price of Bitcoin also depends on aggregate demand.

If a constant supply of money meets a fluctuating aggregate demand, the result is fluctuating prices. In government-run fiat currency systems, the central bank aims to adjust the money supply in response to changes in aggregate demand for money to stabilize the price level. In particular, the Federal Reserve System has been explicitly founded "to provide an elastic currency" to mitigate the price fluctuations that arise from changes in the aggregate demand for the U.S. dollar. Since such a mechanism is absent in the current Bitcoin protocol, the Bitcoin unit will likely display much higher short-term price fluctuations than many government-run fiat currency units.

Mining

The answer to questions on how to make decentralized payment possible, how to make up for the absence of a central authority as a guarantor of currency and transactions and how to guarantee and nurture trust in a system so inherently different from traditional payment systems for the sensitivity to the security of money in Mining.

Often, mistakenly reconnects mining activities to the production and emission of new bitcoins even if this is not the main purpose of this activity. The crucial objective of this process is to maintain the integrity and authenticity of the Blockchain, which for users of the Bitcoin the platform represents a real bank account. Only if this register can maintain the characteristics mentioned above, users can rest assured that that money belongs to them; if instead, it proves to be fragile to counterfeiting attempts, for example, aimed at the validation of several inconsistent transactions (double spending), trust in the system would vanish, and Bitcoin would be doomed to fail.

Anyone can theoretically do the mining activity if a user installs the Bitcoin client on your computer. Mining exploits the computing power of hardware devices made available by network nodes. It is a difficult and time-consuming operation in terms of computer processing times so that new blocks are produced within a fixed time frame, regardless of the number of transactions taking place in the network. If few transactions take place in the network, these cannot be put on hold until a certain threshold is reached, otherwise practicality as a payment system would vanish; moreover, the first mined blocks did not contain any transactions, except the Coinbase, to create and put in circulation the first units of currency.

For each production of a new block, an established quantity of new bitcoins is issued, which belongs to the miner who first produced it. This total quantity also includes the total commissions of the transactions recorded in the block.

In short, Mining was conceived by Nakatomo to secure the Blockchain, and this security is made possible by how many "honest" nodes are present in the network to make the work of "dishonest" nodes difficult, if not impossible. Instead, they want to modify the registry to their advantage to spend more times than the currency already spent.

The honesty of the nodes is "bought" by the same protocol through a specific system of attribution of rewards, which encourage such honesty.

Mining is a specific feature of the Bitcoin platform: other cryptocurrencies, such as for example, Ripple is issued on the market by the company that invented it.

What Is Mining, And How It Works

The production of the new blocks to be attached to the Blockchain and the issue of the emission of new coins are closely linked: in fact, the production of each new block corresponds to the the new issue of a pre-set quantity of bitcoins.

All this process on the Bitcoin platform is clear and established. Regardless of how many transactions occur in the system, every two weeks, an average of 2,016 new blocks must be produced, about 1 every 10 minutes, even in the absence of transactions. Moreover, every two weeks, if the new blocks produced deviate too much from the target number of 2016, the difficulty of producing a new block is revised downwards or upwards, depending on whether the output of new blocks has been lower or above 2,016. Also, the maximum ceiling of bitcoins in circulation is pre-established and is about 21 million units, not yet all in circulation (there are, in fact, 17,232,875 bitcoins in circulation21). Finally, the quantity of new bitcoins emitted at each production of a new one is also a fixed block. This reward originally stood at 50 BTC per block but progressively halved every 210,000 new blocks that equate to approximately 4 years. When the reward is close to zero in the future, the only remuneration for miners will be transaction fees.

It is estimated that in 2040 the reward for each block will be less than 0.5 BTC, so the future of Bitcoin will depend on the diffusion that it will obtain as a payment system, as only if many transactions will take place will the miners be encouraged to continue their activity.

Mining Rules

Mining consists of a set of activities aimed at the correct and constant registration of the transactions that take place in the system. These activities are based on the resolution of a proofof-work, i.e., the task to be performed on your computer that requires processing time.

In particular, Bitcoin imposes the resolution of a cryptographic algorithm very similar to the hashcash function.

Chapter 9: The Cryptocurrencies Economy

The technological innovation introduced by Nakatomi, with Bitcoin, has led to the creation of a real ecosystem around this new payment system. An ecosystem in continuous evolution, formed by different actors concerning the world of traditional payments and new business models generally focused on obtaining and on services concerning the use, exchange and investment of bitcoins or other alternative cryptocurrencies. The economy of these cryptocurrencies are young but in constant turmoil, and several actors gravitate around this world:

☐ **Developers:**

Contribute to the development and improvement of systems from technical point of view and the resolution of the vulnerabilities that are discovered.

☐ **Miners:**

Allow the operation of some systems by validating and registering transactions in the Blockchain, creating and obtaining new units as a reward evaluates according to the methods already described. The profit opportunity offered by Mining has attracted many subjects and many resources, especially since the second half of 2013, which has become a real entrepreneurial activity, thanks also to the introduction in the market of equipment designed specifically For this purpose.

Users:

All the subjects that for different purposes and needs use the various systems, from the merchants who accept them in exchange for goods and services to the people that conserve them for speculative purposes

Wallet services providers:

Provide different types of portfolios electronic, designed for different needs, so that the user can receive, send, or keep bitcoins.

Exchange platforms:

Purchase and sale service in exchange for various legal currencies, other cryptocurrencies, or precious metals. These are generally nonfinancial corporations.

Financial services providers:

Online platforms that offer investment opportunities on cryptocurrency. These subjects facilitate access to the crypto world, facilitating investment in start-ups or specific financial products, from ETFs to derivative products that bet on bitcoins' price trend.

Payment processors:

Services that facilitate the acceptance of cryptocurrencies like means of payment for both physical and online stores, also offering services such as the immediate change in legal currency, to avoid burdening the risk arising from the volatility of the cryptocurrency price in the merchant's financial statements.

Other subjects:

Category of subjects indirectly involved in the environment, but important to identify the overall turnover. Among these can be found companies that manufacture specific hardware for Mining, wallet, and ATMs, those that develop software with different applications in the use of currency, and finally all the start-ups that take advantage of the various technologies, that of the Blockchain as a basis for new applications, different from those of payments.

According to the economic tradition, a currency to be defined as such must satisfy three main functions:

1. Value Reserve:

The currency must be able to preserve its value over time so that users can decide whether to use it immediately or accumulate it to spend it in the future;

2. Means of Exchange:

Money must act as a payment instrument in exchange for goods and services and must be commonly accepted;

3. Unit Of Account:

The currency must perform the function of a common unit of measure, through which to determine the price of goods and facilitate the measurement of economic transactions.

The behavior of bitcoins about the 3 characteristics mentioned above, and it's possible evolution will be described below. It is considered the first function, that is, the value reserve function; it is impossible to establish whether the bitcoin will retain its value in the future. Although there is a limit on the total number of cryptocurrency units in circulation, and this limit together with all the other rules established by the protocol are difficult to distort through substantial modifications, the future demand for bitcoins cannot be predicted with certainty, a real determinant of the price of the cryptocurrency. The future demand for bitcoins will depend on their future use as a payment tool. The bitcoin's value is currently too volatile to be considered an instrument of value reserve, and it is very difficult to predict whether this volatility will persist in the future or if the bitcoin will reach a stable price level.

The medium of exchange function is that the bitcoin seems to be able to satisfy more than all the others, and it is also that for which it has been conceived. With Bitcoin, you can make payments easily, quickly, with high levels of privacy and low costs when compared to all other traditional payment systems. However, cryptocurrency is not universally accepted as a means of payment for goods and services, so it is still difficult to spend them, but there are constantly increasing businesses, both physical and online, willing to accept them.

As seen above, the money volumes exchanged through Bitcoin are only a very small fraction of the total volumes exchanged through the traditional electronic payment systems, and this fraction is even tinier if it is considered that many bitcoin transactions do not concern the purchase of goods or services but are processed only for speculative purposes.

However, even in the context of this second function, it cannot be exempted from considerations regarding the future of Bitcoin. Considering the mining activity and how it is reimbursed, it is necessary to outline the scenarios that could arise in the future when the rewards foresaw for the resolution of each block will be almost nil, and the only profitable source will be represented by the transaction fees: the first possible scenario could be the diffusion of bitcoins as a means of payment could lead to an increase in the number of daily transactions and therefore in the total revenues deriving from commissions, compensating for the cancellation of the rewards for the resolved blocks; the second possible scenario could foresee an increase in the cost of commissions, canceling one of the main advantages deriving from the use of cryptocurrency;

The third possible scenario would be the abandonment of Mining by numerous individuals or companies as it is no longer profitable, with the risk that this activity will be concentrated in the hands of a few subjects or, at worst, degenerate into a monopoly, deleting the most an innovative feature of the system, or the decentralization. Therefore, not even the future use of bitcoins as a means of exchange is so certain, and it is difficult to predict currently.

The last function, the of units of account one, is hardly satisfactory from the bitcoin the current state. The high volatility that characterizes the price of cryptocurrency is not allows easy use as a unit of measurement to determine the value of the assets. Traders should update goods prices in bitcoins even several times throughout the day, since the exchange rate with the dollar or other legal currencies also changes several times on the same day. For this the reason, the prices of the goods remain in any case denominated in legal currency and converted into bitcoins at the time of sale according to the current exchange rate.

From what has emerged so far, can be understood the bitcoins' difficulty in satisfying in exhaustive way of the three functions that are commonly expected from a legal currency, both currently and in the future. Since there is not a central authority that imposes the use or acceptance of bitcoin as a payment instrument, his future can only depend on the will of individuals to use and accept it.

Some doubts hover around the bitcoin and other cryptocurrencies as regards their diffusion. The first is linked to the high price volatility: as already mentioned, the maximum pre-set limit of bitcoin units in circulation (21 million-unit cap) makes its offer curve inelastic, i.e., insensitive to the variations in the cryptocurrency demand of individuals, variations that are reflected in its price.

Even in the hypothesis that the market discovered the the real value of bitcoin as a medium of exchange; however, changes in the demand for bitcoin would determine more or less consistent price fluctuations, considering that the demand can vary due to many factors, for example, to the seasonality of sales or economic cycles. If the offer will be rendered more elastic, increasing or decreasing the rewards for block resolution about the number of transactions processed in a predetermined period or by changing the protocol and introducing new units of money, the effects of changes in demand would reflect the same in price but a less accentuated manner, ensuring greater stability.

Another doubt is related to the possibility that Bitcoin may one day lose its original characteristics. As mentioned earlier, transaction fees may not be enough to reimburse miners' work and generate negative effects, but bitcoin's competitiveness may well persist with some of the traditional payment systems.

Instead, the progressive abandonment of Mining by miners with lower computational powers, which would no longer be able to meet the costs of electricity and maintenance, would focus this activity in the hands of a few individuals, or a single miner that would become a kind of central authority or to carry out a 51% attack as mentioned in the previous chapter; in this situation would appear a real failure of Bitcoin as a a decentralized system, the confidence in the correctness of the Blockchain could be less seen the enormous powers of fraud in the hands of the monopolist, with serious repercussions in the use of cryptocurrency and finally in its value.

In light of what has been analyzed up to now, it can be concluded that bitcoin is very difficult to replace legal currencies in the future since it does not seem able to satisfy the functions of value reserve and unit of account. The bitcoin as a medium of exchange could instead find even wider consents in the future, considering the amount of innovation brought by the phenomenon of cryptocurrencies and Blockchain. Fundamental for this diffusion will be the development of services connected to the world of cryptocurrency, which will offer greater security guarantees and make this world, if possible, even easier and more accessible. The decisions of the Governments regarding the legislative and fiscal qualification to include Bitcoin and the other cryptocurrencies will also be fundamental.

Chapter 10: Cryptocurrency Trading and Market Cap

Cryptocurrency trading is the act of speculating on cryptocurrency price movements via a CFD trading account or buying and selling the underlying coins via an exchange.

CFD Trading On Cryptocurrencies

CFDs trading are derivatives, which enable you to speculate on cryptocurrency price movements without taking ownership of the underlying coins. You can go long ('buy') if you think a cryptocurrency will rise in value or short ('sell') if you think it will fall.

Both are leveraged products, meaning you only need to put up a small deposit – known as margin – to gain full exposure to the underlying market. Your profit or loss are still calculated according to your position's full size so that leverage will magnify both profits and losses.

Buying And Selling Cryptocurrencies Via An Exchange

When you buy cryptocurrencies via an exchange, you purchase the coins themselves. You'll need to create an exchange account, put up the asset's full value to open a position, and store the cryptocurrency tokens in your wallet until you're ready to sell.

Exchanges bring their steep learning curve as you'll need to get to grips with the technology involved and learn how to make sense of the data. Many exchanges also limit how much you can deposit, while accounts can be very expensive to maintain.

How Do Cryptocurrency Markets Work?

Cryptocurrency markets are decentralized, which means they are not issued or backed by a central authority such as a government. Instead, they run across a network of computers. However, cryptocurrencies can be bought and sold via exchanges and stored in 'wallets.'

Unlike traditional currencies, cryptocurrencies exist only as a shared digital record of ownership, stored on a blockchain. When a user wants to send cryptocurrency units to another user, they send it to that user's digital wallet. The transaction isn't considered final until it has been verified and added to the Blockchain through a process called Mining. This is also how new cryptocurrency tokens are usually created.

What Moves Cryptocurrency Markets?

Cryptocurrency markets move according to supply and demand. However, as they are decentralized, they tend to remain free from many economic and political concerns that affect traditional currencies. While there is still a lot of uncertainty surrounding cryptocurrencies, the following factors can have a significant impact on their prices:

Supply: the total number of coins and the rate at which they are released, destroyed, or lost

Market capitalization: the value of all the coins in existence and how users perceive this to be developing

Press: the way the cryptocurrency is portrayed in the media and how much coverage it is getting

Integration: the extent to which the cryptocurrency easily integrates into existing infrastructure such as e-commerce payment systems

Key events: major events such as regulatory updates, security breaches, and economic setbacks

How Does Cryptocurrency Trading Work?

With IG, you can trade cryptocurrencies via a CFD account – derivative products that enable you to speculate on whether your chosen cryptocurrency will rise or fall in value. Prices are quoted in traditional currencies such as the U.S. dollar, and you never take ownership of the cryptocurrency itself.

CFDs are leveraged products, which means you can open a position for just a fraction of the trade's full value. Although leveraged products can magnify your profits, they can magnify losses if the market moves against you.

What Is The Spread In Cryptocurrency Trading?

The spread is the difference between the buy and sell prices quoted for a cryptocurrency. Like many financial markets, you'll be presented with two prices when you open a position on a cryptocurrency market. If you want to open a long position, you trade at the buy price, which is slightly above the market price. If you want to open a short position, you trade at the selling price – slightly below the market price.

What Is A Lot In Cryptocurrency Trading?

Cryptocurrencies are often traded in lots – batches of cryptocurrency tokens are used to standardize trades' size. As cryptocurrencies are very volatile, lots tend to be very small: most are just one unit of the base cryptocurrency. However, some cryptocurrencies are traded in bigger lots.

What Is Leverage In Cryptocurrency Trading?

Leverage is the means of gaining exposure to large amounts of cryptocurrency without having to pay the full value of your trade upfront. Instead, you put down a small deposit, known as margin.

When you close a leveraged position, your profit or loss is based on the trade's full size.

Why Trade Cryptocurrencies?

When you trade cryptocurrencies with I.G., you speculate on whether your chosen market will rise or fall in value without ever taking ownership of the digital asset. This is done by using derivative products such as CFDs.

The Benefits Of Cryptocurrency Trading Include:

Cryptocurrency volatility

Although the cryptocurrency market is relatively new, it has experienced significant volatility due to huge amounts of short-term speculative interest. For example, between October 2017 and October 2018, bitcoin's price rose as high as $19,378 and fell to lows of $5851. Other cryptocurrencies have been comparatively more stable, but new technologies are often likely to attract speculative interest.

The volatility of cryptocurrencies is part of what makes this market so exciting. Rapid intraday price movements can provide a range of opportunities for traders to go long and short and increase risk. If you decide to explore the cryptocurrency market, make sure that you have done your research and developed a risk management strategy.

Cryptocurrency Market Hours

The cryptocurrency market is usually available to trade 24 hours a day, seven days a week because there is no centralized market governance. Cryptocurrency transactions take place directly between individuals on cryptocurrency exchanges all over the world. However, there may be periods of downtime when the market adjusts to infrastructural updates or 'forks.'

With IG, you can trade cryptocurrencies against fiat currencies – such as the U.S. dollar –

Improved Liquidity

Liquidity is the measure of how quickly and easily a cryptocurrency can be converted into cash without impacting the market price. Liquidity is important because it brings about better pricing, faster transaction times, and increased technical analysis accuracy.

In general, the cryptocurrency market is considered illiquid because the transactions are dispersed across multiple exchanges, which means that comparatively small trades can significantly impact market prices. This is part of the reason cryptocurrency markets are so volatile.

However, when you trade cryptocurrency CFDs with I.G., you can get improved liquidity because we source prices from multiple venues on your behalf. This means that your trades are more likely to be executed quickly and at a lower cost.

Ability To Go Long Or Short

When you buy a cryptocurrency, you are purchasing the asset upfront, hoping to increase value. But when you trade on the price of a cryptocurrency, you can take advantage of markets that are falling in price, as well as rising. This is known as going short.

1. Short Selling
2. Going long

For example, let's say that you have decided to open a short CFD position on Ether's price there you believe that the market is going to fall. If you were right, and the value of Ether fEthergainst the U.S. dollar, your trade would profit. However, if the value of Ether rEthergainst the U.S. dollar, your position would be making a loss.

Leveraged Exposure

As CFD trading is a leveraged product, it enables you to open a position on 'margin' – a deposit worth just a fraction of the trade's full value. In other words, you could gain a large exposure to a cryptocurrency market while only tying up a relatively small amount of your capital.

The profit or loss you make from your cryptocurrency trades will reflect the full value of the position at the point it is closed, so trading on margin offers you the opportunity to make large profits from a relatively small investment. However, it can also amplify any losses, including losses that could exceed your initial deposit for the individual trade. This is why it is crucial to consider the total value of the leveraged position before trading CFDs.

It is also important to ensure that you have a suitable risk management strategy in place, which should include the appropriate stops and limits.

Faster Account Opening

When you buy cryptocurrencies, you'll need to buy and sell via an exchange, which requires you to create an exchange account and store the cryptocurrency in your digital wallet. This process can be restrictive and time-consuming.

But when cryptocurrency trading with I.G., you won't need access to the exchange directly because we're exposed to the underlying market on your behalf. You won't need to set up and manage an exchange account so that you could be set up and ready to trade much more quickly. You could be trading in less than five minutes with our simple application form and instant online verification.

What Is The Leverage?

Leverage enables you to gain a large exposure to a financial market while only tying up a relatively small amount of your capital. In this way, leverage magnifies the scope for both gains and losses.

Is Leveraged Dealing Risky?

Even though you only put up a relatively small amount of capital to open a position, your profit or loss is based on the full value of the position. Therefore, the amount you gain or lose could be relatively large compared to your initial outlay.

Protect Against Adverse Movements For Free

Set a stop-loss to close your position automatically if the market moves against you. There's no trigger charge but no guarantee of protection against slippage – so your position could be closed out at a worse level if the market gaps.

Choose Exactly Where Your Trade Closes.

Attach a guaranteed stop to your position, and it'll always be closed out at exactly the price you specified.

What's more, you'll only pay for your stop if it's triggered. If this happens, our guaranteed stop premiums offer excellent value in the market for most major indices and F.X. pairs.

Don't miss out on profits.

Place a trailing stop when you open your trade, and it will move with your profit. If the market turns, your position will close out at your trailing stop's new level. So you can lock in profits without the need to monitor your position and adjust your stop. Like regular stop-losses, trailing stops don't protect against slippage.

Take Profit Automatically

Set a limit order in line with your profit target, and we'll close your position for you when the price hits your chosen level.

Stay On Top Of Market Movement.

Set price alerts, and we'll notify you by text or email when a market reaches your specified price. Push alert notifications can also be set and are free. They can be set up on our web-based platform and our apps. Unlike text and email alerts, push alerts pop up on the trading platform when using a P.C. and on your mobile when using our apps.

Always Know Your Profit And Loss.

Keep an eye on the always-visible balance snapshot in our platform, react quickly if the market moves against you, and deal out almost instantly to protect a profit or minimize a loss.

What Is The Market Cap Of A Cryptocurrency?

Crypto market capitalization or "crypto market cap" for short is a widely used metric used to compare the relative size of different cryptocurrencies. On CoinCodex, the market cap is the default metric by which we rank cryptocurrencies on our front page. We also track the total cryptocurrency market cap by adding the market cap of all the cryptocurrencies listed on CoinCodex. The total market cap provides an estimate of whether the cryptocurrency market as a whole is growing or declining.

How Is The Crypto Market Cap Calculated?

We calculate a cryptocurrency's market cap by taking the cryptocurrency's Price per unit and multiplying it with the cryptocurrency's circulating supply. The formula is simple: Market Cap = Price * Circulating Supply. Circulating supply refers to the number of units of a cryptocurrency currently existing and can be transacted with.

Let's quickly calculate the market cap of Bitcoin as an example. The Bitcoin price is currently $32,109, and there are 18.59 million BTC coins in circulation. If we use the above formula, we multiply the two numbers and arrive at a market cap of $596.95 billion.

Does Market Cap Matter In Cryptocurrency?

Crypto market cap matters because it is a useful way to compare different cryptocurrencies. If Coin A has a significantly higher market cap than Coin B, this tells us that Coin A is likely adopted more widely by individuals and businesses and valued higher by the market. On the other hand, it could also indicate that Coin B is undervalued relative to Coin A.

Even though the market cap is a widely used metric, it can sometimes be misleading. A good rule of thumb is that the usefulness of any given cryptocurrency's market cap metric increases in proportion with the cryptocurrency's trading volume. Suppose a cryptocurrency is actively traded and has deep liquidity across many different exchanges. In that case, it becomes much harder for single actors to manipulate prices and create an unrealistic market cap for the cryptocurrency.

How Can A Cryptocurrency Increase Its Market Cap?

A cryptocurrency's market cap increases when its Price per unit increases. Alternatively, an increase in circulating supply can also lead to an increase in the market cap. However, an increase in supply also tends to lead to a lower price per unit, and the two cancel each other out to a large extent. In practice, an increase in Price per unit is the main way a cryptocurrency's market cap grows.

What Is Bitcoin's Market Cap?

The Bitcoin market cap is currently $596.95 billion. We arrive at this figure by multiplying the Price of 1 BTC and the circulating supply of Bitcoin. The Bitcoin price is currently $32,109, and its circulating supply is 18.59 million. If we multiply these two numbers, we arrive at a market cap of $596.95 billion.

What Is Cryptocurrency Circulating Supply?

The circulating supply of a cryptocurrency is the number of units that are currently available for use. Let's use Bitcoin as an example. There is a rule in the Bitcoin code, which says that only 21 million Bitcoins can ever be created. The circulating supply of Bitcoin started at 0 but immediately started growing as new blocks were mined and new BTC coins were being created to reward the miners. Currently, there are around 18.52 million Bitcoins in existence, and this number will keep growing until the 21 millionths BTC is mined. Since 18.59 million BTC have been mined so far, we say that this is the circulating supply of Bitcoin.

What Is An Altcoin?

An altcoin is any cryptocurrency that is not Bitcoin. The word "altcoin" is short for "alternative coin", and is commonly used by cryptocurrency investors and traders to refer to all coins other than Bitcoin. Thousands of altcoins have been created so far following Bitcoin's launch in 2009.

What Is The Difference Between Bitcoin And Altcoins?

Bitcoin is the oldest and most established cryptocurrency and has a larger market cap than all other cryptocurrencies combined. Bitcoin is also the most widely adopted cryptocurrency and is accepted by practically all businesses that deal with cryptocurrency.

However, Bitcoin is far from the only player in the game, and numerous altcoins have reached multi-billion dollar valuations. The second-largest cryptocurrency is Ethereum, which supports smart contracts and allows users to make highly complex decentralized applications. Ethereum has grown so large that the word "altcoin" is rarely used to describe it now.

Generally, altcoins attempt to improve upon the basic design of Bitcoin by introducing technology that is absent from Bitcoin. This includes privacy technologies, different distributed ledger architectures, and consensus mechanisms.

What Is A Stable Coin?

A stablecoin is a crypto asset that maintains a stable value regardless of market conditions. This is most commonly achieved by pegging the stablecoin to a specific fiat currency such as the US dollar. Stablecoins are useful because they can still be transacted on blockchain networks while avoiding the price volatility of "normal" cryptocurrencies such as Bitcoin and Ethereum. Outside of stablecoins, cryptocurrency prices can change rapidly, and it's not uncommon to see the crypto market gain or lose more than 10% in a single day.

Now, let's provide a simple theoretical example of how stable coins' value stays stable.

Let's say that a company creates Stablecoin X (SCX), which is designed to trade as closely to $1 as possible at all times. The company will hold USD reserves equal to the number of SCX tokens in circulation and provide users the option to redeem 1 SCX token for $1. If the Price of SCX is lower than $1, demand for SCX will increase because traders will buy it and redeem it for a profit.

This will drive the Price of SCX back towards $1.

Tether's USDT was the first stable coin ever launched and is still the most popular option on the market.

What Is Defi?

Defi (decentralized finance) refers to a wide variety of decentralized applications that enable financial services such as lending, borrowing, and trading. Defi applications are built on top of blockchain platforms such as Ethereum and allow anyone to access these financial services simply by using their cryptocurrency wallets.

To give you a better idea of what kind of use cases are enabled by Defi applications, let's quickly go through some major Defi apps and what they accomplish:

- **Maker:** Users can post their cryptocurrencies as collateral to receive a loan in the form of Dai stablecoins
- **Compound:** Users can borrow cryptocurrency or loan out their cryptocurrency to earn interest • **Uniswap:** Users can swap between different Ethereum-based tokens in a decentralized manner
- **DYdX:** A decentralized platform where users can go long or short on cryptocurrencies

Chapter 11: Blockchain and the Banking System

Blockchain is transforming everything from payment transactions to how money is raised in the private market. Will the traditional banking industry embrace this technology or be replaced by it?

Where Is This Data Coming From?

Email

Blockchain technology has received a lot of attention over the last few years, propelling beyond the praise of niche Bitcoin fanatics and into banking experts and investors' mainstream conversation.

Last September, JPMorgan Chase CEO Jamie Dimon took a stab at Bitcoin: "It's worse than tulip bulbs. It won't end well. Someone is going to get killed." Lloyd Blankfein, head of Goldman Sachs, echoed that thought, saying, "Something that moves 20% [overnight] does not feel like a currency. It is a vehicle to perpetrate fraud."

Despite the skepticism, whether blockchain and decentralized ledger technology (DLT) will replace or revolutionize elements of the banking system remains.

And this very loud and public backlash against cryptocurrencies from banks begs another question:

What do banks have to be afraid of?

Blockchain's Role In Banking

Blockchain technology provides a way for untrusted parties to agree on a database's state without using a middleman. By providing a ledger that nobody administers, a blockchain could provide specific financial services — like payments or securitization — without using a middleman, like a bank.

Further, blockchain allows for the use of tools like "smart contracts," which could potentially automate manual processes, from compliance and claims processing to distributing the contents of a will.

For use cases that don't need a high degree of decentralization — but could benefit from better coordination — blockchain's cousin, "distributed ledger technology (DLT)," could help corporates establish better governance standards around data sharing and collaboration.

With global banking currently, a $134T industry, blockchain technology, and DLT could disintermediate key services that banks provide, including:

Payments: By establishing a decentralized ledger for payments (e.g., Bitcoin), blockchain technology could facilitate faster payments at lower fees than banks.

Clearance and Settlement Systems: Distributed ledgers can reduce operational costs and bring us closer to real-time transactions between financial institutions.

Fundraising: Initial Coin Offerings (ICOs) experiment with a new financing model that unbundles access to capital from traditional capital-raising services and firms.

Securities: By tokenizing traditional securities such as stocks, bonds, and alternative assets and placing them on public blockchains — blockchain technology could create more efficient, interoperable capital markets.

Loans and Credit: By removing the need for gatekeepers in the loan and credit industry, blockchain technology can make it more secure to borrow money and provide lower interest rates.

Trade Finance: By replacing the cumbersome, paper-heavy bills of lading process in the trade finance industry, blockchain technology can create more transparency, security, and trust among trade parties globally.

Read on for a deep dive into how blockchain technology could turn the traditional banking industry on its head while enabling new business models through technology.

1. Payments

Blockchain technology offers a high-security, low-cost way of sending payments that cut down on the need for verification from third parties and beats processing times for traditional bank transfers 90% of members of the European Payments Council believe blockchain technology will fundamentally change the industry by 2025

Today, trillions of dollars are sloshing worldwide via an antiquated system of slow payments and added fees.

If you work in San Francisco and want to send part of your paycheck back to your family in

London, you might have to pay a $25 flat fee for a wire transfer, and additional fees adding up to 7%. Your bank gets a cut, the receiving bank gets a cut, and you're charged exchange rate fees.

Your family's bank might not even register the transaction until a week later.

Despite more recent fluctuations, the number of confirmed Bitcoin transactions per day has grown roughly 6x from just over 50,000 in the summer of 2014 to ~290,000 as of December 2018. Source:

Blockchain.

Facilitating payments is highly profitable for banks, providing them with little incentive to lower fees. From payments to letters of credit, cross-border transactions generated 40% of global payments transactional revenues during 2016.

Cryptocurrencies like Bitcoin and Ethereum are built on public blockchains that anyone can use to send and receive money. In this way, public blockchains cut down on the need for trusted third parties to verify transactions and give people worldwide access to fast, cheap, and borderless payments.

Bitcoin transactions can take 30 minutes or up to 16 hours — in extreme cases — to settle. That's still not perfect, but it represents a leg up from the average 3-day processing time for bank transfers. And due to their decentralized and complex nature, crypto-based transactions are difficult for governments and regulatory bodies to control. In other words, they can't shut down these almostinstantaneous transactions.

More importantly, developers are working on scaling cheaper solutions for cryptocurrencies — like Bitcoin and Ethereum — to process more transactions faster. Other cryptocurrencies, like Bitcoin Cash and TRON, already have low-priced transactions.

Examples of Improved Payments Through Blockchain

While cryptocurrencies are a long way from completely replacing fiat (like the US dollar) when it comes to payments, the last couple of years have seen mostly upward growth in transaction volume for cryptocurrencies Bitcoin and Ethereum.

Some companies are using blockchain technology to improve B2B payments in developing economies. One example of this is BitPesa; a blockchain company focused on facilitating B2B payments in countries like Kenya, Nigeria, and Uganda. The company has processed millions of dollars in transactions, reportedly growing 20% month-over-month.

2. Clearance and Settlements Systems

Takeaways

☐ Distributed ledger technology could allow transactions to be settled directly and keep track of transactions better than existing protocols, like SWIFT.

☐ Among others, Ripple and R3 are working with traditional banks to bring greater efficiency to the sector.

The fact that an average bank transfer — as described above — takes three days to settle has a lot to do with the way our financial infrastructure was built.

It's not just a pain for the consumer. Moving money around the world is a logistical nightmare for the banks themselves. Today, a simple bank transfer — from one account to another — has to bypass a complicated system of intermediaries, from correspondent banks to custodial services, before it ever reaches any destination. The two bank balances have to be reconciled across a global financial system, comprised of a wide network of traders, funds, asset managers, and more.

Suppose you want to send money from a UnicaCredit Banca account in Italy to a Wells Fargo account in the US. In that case, the transfer will be executed through the Society for Worldwide Interbank Financial Communication (SWIFT) send 24 million messages a day to 10,000 financial institutions.

Because UnicaCredit Banka and Wells Fargo don't have an established financial relationship, they have to search the SWIFT network for a correspondent bank with a relationship with both banks and settle the transaction fee. Each correspondent bank maintains different ledgers at the originating bank and the receiving bank, which means that these different ledgers have to be reconciled at the end of the day.

The centralized SWIFT protocol doesn't send the funds; it simply sends the payment orders. The actual money is then processed through a system of intermediaries. Each intermediary adds additional cost to the transaction and creates a potential point of failure — 60% of B2B payments require manual intervention, each taking between 15-20 minutes.

Blockchain technology, which serves as a decentralized "ledger" of transactions, could disrupt this state of play. Rather than using SWIFT to reconcile each financial institution's ledger, an interbank blockchain could publicly and transparently keep track of all transactions. That means that instead of having to rely on a network of custodial services and correspondent banks, transactions could be settled directly on a public blockchain.

Further, blockchain technology allows for "atomic" transactions or transactions that clear and settle when a payment is made. This stands in contrast to current banking systems, which clear and settles a transaction days after payment.

That might help alleviate the high costs of maintaining a global network of correspondent banks. Banks have estimated that blockchain innovation could cut at least $20B worth of costs from the financial sector by providing better infrastructure for clearance and settlements.

3. Fundraising

Takeaways

☐ In initial coin offerings (ICOs), entrepreneurs raise money by selling tokens or coins, allowing them to fundraise without a traditional investor or VC firm (and the due diligence that accompanies an investment from one)

☐ Blockchain company EOS raised over \$4B in its year-long ICO ending in 2018.

Raising money through venture capital is an arduous process. Entrepreneurs put together decks, sit through countless meetings with partners, and endure long negotiations over equity and valuation in the hopes of exchanging some chunk of their company for a check.

In contrast, some companies raise funds via "initial coin offerings (ICOs)," powered by public blockchains like Ethereum and Bitcoin.

In an ICO, projects sell tokens, or coins, in exchange for funding (often denominated in Bitcoin or ether). The token value is — at least in theory — tied to the success of the blockchain company. Investing in tokens is a way for investors to bet directly on usage and value. Through ICOs, blockchain companies can short-circuit the conventional fundraising process by selling tokens directly to the public.

Some high-profile ICOs have raised hundreds of millions — even billions — of dollars before proof of a viable product. Filecoin, a blockchain data storage startup, raised \$257M, while EOS, building a "world computer," raised over \$4B in its year-long ICO. Still, regulators are putting a serious damper on ICOs.

At the same time, initial coin offerings represent a paradigm shift in how companies finance development.

First, ICOs occur globally and online, giving companies access to an exponentially larger pool of investors. You're no longer limited to high-net-worth individuals, institutions, and others who can show the government that they're credible investors.

Second, ICOs gives companies immediate access to liquidity. The moment you sell a token, it's priced on a 24-hour global market. Compare that to ten years for venture-backed startups. As Earn CEO Balaji Srinivasan says, "the ratio between 10 years and 10 minutes to get the option of liquidity is up to a 500,000x speedup in time." We already see the impact of ICOs on the fundraising market.

Venture capital firms have taken notice, with Sequoia, Andreessen Horowitz, and Union Square Ventures, all directly investing in ICOs, and gaining exposure by investing in cryptocurrency hedge funds.

Venrock partner David Pakman has said, "There's no question that crypto will disrupt the business of venture capital. And I hope it does. The democratization of everything is what has excited me about technology from the beginning."

4. Securities

Takeaways

☐ Blockchain removes the middleman in asset rights transfers, low asset exchange fees, gives access to wider global markets, and reduces the instability of the traditional securities market.
☐ Moving securities on the blockchain could save $17B to $24B per year in global trade processing costs.

To buy or sell assets like stocks, debt, and commodities, you need a way to keep track of who owns what. Today, financial markets accomplish this through a complex chain of brokers, exchanges, central security depositories, clearinghouses, and custodian banks. These different parties have been built around an outdated system of paper ownership that is not only slow but can be inaccurate and prone to deception.

Say you want to buy a share of Apple stock. You might place an order through a stock exchange, which matches you with a seller. In the old days, that meant you'd spend cash exchanging for a certificate of ownership for the share.

This grows a lot more complicated when we're trying to execute this transaction electronically. We don't want to deal with the day-to-day management of the assets — like exchanging certificates, bookkeeping, or managing dividends. So we outsource the shares to custodian banks for safekeeping. Because buyers and sellers don't always rely on the same custodian banks, the custodians themselves need to rely on a trusted third party to hold onto all the paper certificates.

5. Loans And Credit

Takeaways

☐ Blockchain-enabled lending offers a more secure way of offering personal loans to a larger pool of consumers and would make the loan process cheaper, more efficient, and more secure.

☐ The first live securities lending took place in 2018 with a $30.48M transaction between Credit Suisse and ING.

The worlds of the consumer, the financial institution, and blockchain are slowly converging. Another space where that convergence can completely upend the way finance operates today is lending and credit.

Traditional banks and lenders underwrite loans based on a system of credit reporting. Blockchain technology opens up the possibility of peer-to-peer loans, complex programmed loans that can approximate a mortgage or syndicated loan structure, and a faster and more secure loan process in general.

When you fill out an application for a bank loan, the bank must evaluate the risk that you won't pay them back. They do this by looking at factors like your credit score, debt-to-income ratio, and homeownership status. To get this information, they have to access your credit report from one of three major credit agencies: Experian, TransUnion, and Equifax.

Banks price the risk of default into the fees and interest collected on loans based on that information.

6. Trade Finance

Takeaways

- ☐ Blockchain and distributed ledger technology (DLT) can support cross-border trade transactions that would otherwise be uneconomical because of costs related to trade and documentation processes. It would also shorten delivery times and reduce paper use.
- ☐ With approximately 80 to 90% of world trade relying on trade finance, blockchain's influence on the market would be felt globally throughout all industries that use crossborder trading.

Trade finance exists to mitigate risks, extend credit, and ensure that exporters and importers can engage in international trade.

It is a pivotal part of the global financial system, yet it frequently operates on antiquated, manual, and written documentation. Blockchain represents the opportunity to streamline and simplify the complex world of trade finance, saving importers, exporters, and financiers billions of dollars every year.

Blockchain technology has had an increasingly regular presence in trade programs for a year now, but its mainstream role in lading and credit bills has only recently begun to firm.

Like many industries, the trade finance market has suffered from logistical setbacks due to old, outdated, and uneconomical manual documentation processes for years. Physical letters of credit, given by one party's bank to the other party's bank, are still often used to ensure that payment will be received.

By enabling companies to securely and digitally prove country of origin, product, and transaction details (and any other documentation), Blockchain technology could help exporters and importers provide each other with more visibility into the shipments moving through their pipelines and more assurance of delivery.

One of the greatest risks to trade parties is the threat of fraud, which is greater because of a lack of confidentiality and little oversight on the flow of goods and documentation. This opens up the possibility of the same shipment being repeatedly mortgaged, an unfortunate occurrence that happens so often that commodity trade finance banks write it off as a cost of business.

Through blockchain technology, payments between importers and exporters could occur in tokenized form contingent upon delivery or receipt of goods. Through smart contracts, importers and exporters could set up rules that would ensure automatic payments and cut out the possibility of missing, lapsed, or repeatedly mortgaged shipments.

Unfortunately, there are many ways that some Internet users exploit unsecured computing systems to mine or steal cryptocurrency. Learn more about staying safe and protecting yourself in this emerging market before you start investing in cryptocurrency.

Chapter 12: Cryptocurrencies and Taxes

Cryptocurrency is a digital currency, or a "digital representation of value," as the IRS puts it. You can't see it, hold it in your hand, or put it in your wallet. It's been in use for over a decade and has grown in popularity over the last few years. Instead of using a bank to create, transfer, and exchange funds, cryptocurrency employs a distributed, encrypted blockchain network to process transactions. No bank or government authority controls it as they do with traditional currencies.

So, if you have used cryptocurrency this year, what are the implications for filing your taxes?

A Cryptocurrency Primer

First of all, let's make sure we're all on the same page regarding this new kind of money. Cryptocurrency units are referred to as coins, even though there's no physical coin. You store cash in a digital wallet or use an exchange or brokerage. Significant providers of these include Coinbase, Kraken, Binance, and Jaxx. Bitcoin was the first cryptocurrency, and it remains the most popular, though it's been joined by Ethereum and Litecoin, among others. Cryptocurrency can be used to pay for goods or services, invest, or exchange funds with someone else. The coins can also be exchanged for traditional currency. You can find real-time exchange prices for Bitcoin here. Cryptocurrency transactions are recorded in an anonymized blockchain, which can be thought of as a digitized public ledger.

This form of money is still in its infancy, so don't expect to use it for online shopping, though some vendors have started accepting it. It's relatively popular among online gambling sites, and you could even buy a Lamborghini with it. Some employers have begun paying employees with it; the dollar value of the cryptocurrency at the time of the transaction is treated as W-2 or 1099 income. The mechanics of using cryptocurrency are often as simple as scanning a QR code or copy and pasting a long ID, but what happens in the background is far more involved than your typical bank transaction since the transaction has to be verified by lots of distributed servers, rather than one bank or exchange.

Cryptocurrency As Property

If you've been using cryptocurrency but not paying taxes on its related transactions, you're not alone. You're also not compliant with IRS regulations, which could catch up with you someday. The agency may penalize you unless you can prove "reasonable cause."

Since 2014, the IRS has considered cryptocurrency to be property. Taxpayers are required to report transactions involving virtual currency like US dollars on their tax returns, which means they must determine its fair market value as of the transaction date. You can determine fair market value by converting the virtual currency into US dollars or into another cash that can then be converted into

US dollars (assuming the currency's exchange rate is established by market supply and demand).

You need to do some exact bookkeeping if you're planning to use cryptocurrency. Several accounting solutions are designed for this, but QuickBooks may work just fine for you (with some workarounds). It would help if you started keeping detailed records from the start since reconstructing years of transactions could be difficult or even impossible.

Does this mean you could be on the hook for transactions going back to 2014? Yes. The IRS sent letters last year to taxpayers who'd been involved in cryptocurrency transactions, informing them that they had to file amended returns and pay back taxes. It's also released a new form for the 2019 tax year. The Schedule 1 now includes the following phrase above Part I: Additional Income: "At any time during 2019, did you receive, sell, send, exchange, or otherwise acquire any financial interest in any virtual currency?"

Capital Assets And Cryptocurrency

If you sell your home because you're moving or some stocks because you want to take your profit, these properties are considered capital assets. It's similar to virtual currencies. You pay capital gains taxes on them—either short (held less than a year, and taxed as ordinary income) or long term—on your Schedule D. These are calculated just like other capital gains and losses: You take your cost basis (the amount you paid for the currency) and figure how much it's gone up or down since that date. Capital gains rates for the 2019 tax year can be 0, 15, or 20 percent, depending on your taxable income.

However, if you're selling property as a part of a business or trade, the property is not considered a capital asset and is taxed as ordinary income. This applies to virtual currency sales, too. The IRS looks at the "character" of the gain or loss—your intent, or why you're selling.

Cryptocurrency And Turbotax

TurboTax (buy) is the only tax preparation website that walks you through the process of recording a cryptocurrency sale. It does so thoroughly and with lots of guidance. This tax topic is not included in the Deluxe version, though. You'll have to spring for Premier or Self-Employed.

You can find the cryptocurrency mini-wizard under Investment Income. Four situations would require you to complete this section. You'd do so if you:

- ☐ Sold cryptocurrency
- ☐ Converted cryptocurrency to a conventional currency like US dollars
- ☐ Exchanged one of the various types of cryptocurrency for another one
- ☐ Used cryptocurrency to purchase products or services

Cryptocurrency transactions are sometimes reported on Form 1099-B, Form 1099-K, or a tax statement that your exchange sent to you. Businesses are not required to send these forms out, so don't be surprised if you don't have one from 2019. It's your responsibility to keep track of your transactions. You can do so by downloading your order or trading history from your exchange's website as a CSV file. If you're a frequent trader, you should be doing this at periodic intervals throughout the year since your business may limit you to three months of data, for example. You'll also be able to enter the data manually.

TurboTax allows you to download CSV files from eight cryptocurrency services: Coinbase, Bitcoin.Tax, BitTaxer, CoinTracker, CryptoTrader.Tax, Robinhood, TokenTax, and ZenLedger.

You can either drag and drop your files or browse your system for them.

When you enter your data manually, TurboTax needs the service name, asset name (like Bitcoin or Ethereum), purchase date, cost basis, sale date, and sale proceeds. You may have to contact your exchange if your CSV files' labels don't match those in TurboTax exactly. The site provides the fields you'll need to complete for each transaction on one screen.

After you enter this data and click Continue, a summary of the transaction will appear. You can either add more transactions or continue with the return if you're finished. A final summary tells you whether it was a short-term or long-term gain or loss and if the transaction will be reported on your tax return.

Chapter 13: Present and future of Bitcoin

We live in a world where our online IDs are in the hands of the government, social media, and banks, and we rely on them to keep us secure. Blockchain IDs put you and only you in control. Therefore, you can store all of your passwords and any other personal information securely on the blockchain, eliminating the need for passwords in everything from Skype to Facebook, Twitter, and more. These ID services could be applied to government services, medicine, and any other record-keeping agency in the future.

The blockchain system's real potential comes from its foundation of decentralization, transparency, and an unrestricted market. It exists to combat greed and middlemen and to give individuals ultimate control of their identity and activity. In a foreseeable blockchain future, we will see a world where our medical records are immediately available if we are in an accident, where online voting was possible; and transparency was paramount, and greed is disincentivized.

Can Blockchain Change The World?

Before we decide to answer the question at our disposal, we first need to understand the blockchain's idea.

The first sector that will see the change in the financial industry. The finance sector is going through significant problems right now. It requires disruption to survive. Blockchain can be the perfect catalyst and solution that can provide the necessary means to solve the blockchain industry's pains.

Blockchain changes how money flows through institutions or is traded among traders.

Blockchain has the potential to change almost every industry out there. It can create a more efficient and prosperous world where people can connect without the need for intermediaries.

Companies can also utilize blockchain technology to provide a more transparent, trustworthy, and efficient service to the consumer. For instance, a company can use a permissioned network to create an efficient system. They can also utilize it to keep transparency with the end-user by sharing information to build trust among users.

As for general users, they can also utilize the blockchain to its full potential. If you are a creator, you can connect with the buyers directly using a blockchain solution. At this moment, we can't predict correctly when exactly blockchain will take over, but we do know that the process has already started.

How Blockchain Will Change The Financial World?

The financial world will be changed entirely with the help of the blockchain. Blockchain platforms can transform the global economy quite quickly.

For example, the Ethereum blockchain can automate, secure, and operate an efficient process in the finance and banking sector. It will also optimize cost and digitize securities and other assets without increasing the cost required to manage them.

The financial world can always benefit from the transparency, trust, privacy, scalability, and security that blockchain offers. For instance, the financial market can utilize programming capabilities and automate things such as KYC/AML, data privacy, etc. It can also help streamline processes with improved efficiency.

Blockchain will succeed in changing the financial sector as it's way more superior to the transactional model.

Some of the best blockchain use-cases in the financial world include the following.

- ☐ Investment management
- ☐ Lending and banking
- ☐ Insurance
- ☐ Trade finance

How Blockchain Will Change Real Estate?

Have you ever tried to buy a home recently? Then, you would know how much effort and time you need to complete a purchase. Any real estate transaction can take anywhere between a few weeks to months to complete. The reason behind the delay is the use of a less efficient all-together process.

The large scale of the real estate makes it very hard for buyers and sellers to coordinate and manage their properties.

With blockchain, real estate can see many changes, including bringing in a more efficient process with automation. Other benefits include real-time payment settlements, reduced costs, tokenization, and real-time payment settlements. This is a massive boost that can help blockchain transform the global economy.

The most significant advantage is the reduced time it takes to make deals. With proper tokenization, real-world assets can be stored and traded on the blockchain. Tokenization also means that other kinds of information can be reserved online, including real estate funds, governance rights, and more!

Few of the blockchain use-cases in real estate include the following:

☐ Deed records and Land titles
☐ Tokenization
☐ Leasing and payments
☐ Real-time accounting
☐ Tenant identity

Curious about blockchain's impact on real estate? Check out our guide on blockchain for real estate right now!

How Blockchain Will Change HealthCare?

The last sector that we are going to discuss is the HealthCare. Right now, healthcare can also benefit from the blockchain. There are many pain points in the healthcare industry. For example, patients have always had to carry their documents with them. This can lead to issues including wrong data input.

Another thing that needs to be fixed is drug traceability. With no proper traceability, drugs can be counterfeited easily. Research is also hampered, considering that patients' data is not accessible for the most part.

Few of the blockchain use-cases in healthcare include the following:

- Drug traceability
- Patient consent management
- Electronic Health Records(EHRs)
- Better clinical trials

Will Blockchain Succeed?

The path of making blockchain global and reaching everyone around the world is not easy. Blockchain seems promising, just like any other new technology out there. When the internet came along, it caused ripples and hailed as the single most revolutionary technology out there. It did change how we connect, but it took its own time to evolve and improve.

Artificial Intelligence was also hailed as the next-generation technology that can change the world. My point is that almost every new technology shows promise as they are better than the previous ones in one way or another. Only time can tell how blockchain will impact society. For now, everyone is on the same page. But, for sure, blockchain is very promising and has the potential to change the world around us.

However, what things can go wrong with the overall bright vision for blockchain technology? One of the biggest hurdles that need to be taken care of is governance. As blockchain is decentralized, governing it can be a very tricky situation. As it is currently in a growth stage, it can be used for naughty or harmful things. The main focus should be to create a governing body that can dictate safe rules and regulations for using blockchain technology. This way, we can ensure that blockchain technology is used in the right way.

So, it is tough to say what direction blockchain will take firmly. Its impacts have already been seen in many use-cases discussed above, but the adoption rates are still struggling.

Conclusion

Cryptocurrency is an exciting concept with the power to fundamentally alter global finance for the better. But while it's based on sound, democratic principles, cryptocurrency remains a technological and practical work in progress. For the foreseeable future, nation-states' nearmonopoly on currency production and monetary policy appears secure.

In the meantime, cryptocurrency users (and nonusers intrigued by cryptocurrency's promise) need to remain ever-mindful of the concept's practical limitations. Any claims that a particular cryptocurrency confers total anonymity or immunity from legal accountability are worthy of deep skepticism, claiming that individual cryptocurrencies represent foolproof investment opportunities or inflation hedges. After all, gold is often touted as the ultimate inflation hedge, yet it's still subject to wild volatility – more so than many first-world fiat currencies.

The volatility also remains a concern for large, conservative investors who would struggle to justify adding an asset that regularly notches-up daily moves of above 10 percent and whose features are unlikely to make bitcoin a must for investors who are unfavorable to risk.

Personal Notes